# TONGASS NATIONAL FOREST
*A Temperate Rainforest in Transition*

Mendenhall Glacier, Juneau

*Everybody needs beauty as well as bread, places to…*

Above Sockeye Falls, Taku Inlet

...*play in and pray in, where nature may heal and give*...

Awaiting restoration, Totem Bight State Historical Park

...*strength to body and soul alike.* — *John Muir*

Salmon River, Hyder

# TONGASS NATIONAL FOREST
*A Temperate Rainforest in Transition*

By Andromeda Romano-Lax

Alaska Geographic Association
Anchorage, Alaska

The publisher thanks the Tongass National Forest for their assistance in developing and reviewing this publication. Alaska Geographic works in partnership with the National Forest Service to further public education and appreciation for the national forests in Alaska.

**Author:** Andromeda Romano-Lax

**Photography:** Alaska State Library, A.K. McDaniel Photograph Collection, P120-018, page: 54; © Daniel Buckscott/WildernessPeaks.com, pages: 86-87; © Carr Clifton, page: 50 inset, 82; Jon Cornforth, page: 34; Stephen Dalton, pages: 22-23; © 2011 Willie G. Dalton, page: 72; Carl Donohue, page: 100 inset; © Patrick J. Endres/AlaskaPhotographics.com, pages: 2-3, 6-7, 78-79, back cover inset; Patrick Endres/AlaskaStock.com, pages: 47, 63; John Gomes, page: 32; Loyd C. Heath, pages: vi-vii; Fred Hirschmann, pages: cover, i, viii-ix, 13, 27, 35 inset, 52, 64-65, 76, 89, 96-97; John Hyde, pages: cover flaps, ii-iii, iv-v, 8, 9, 10-11, 14-15, 16, 18, 20 inset, 20-21 background, 24, 26, 28-29, 31, 33, 34-35 background, 36-37, 44-45, 56, 67, 68-69, 70-71 background, 88, 90, 91, 92 inset, 92-93 background, 95, 100 background, back cover; Mark Kelly, pages: 80, 98-99; Mark Kelly/AlaskaStock.com, page: 25; © 2011 www.robertglennketchum.com, pages: 4-5, 12; Robert Lowe, page: xi, 30, 70 inset, 71 inset; Ernest Manewal/AlaskaStock.com, page: 46; Clark James Mishler, pages: 48-49; Clark James Mishler/AlaskStock.com, pages: 60-61; © Ron Niebrugge/wildnatureimages.com, pages: 7, 51 inset, 73, 75; Marion Owen dba Carotte, Inc./AlaskaStock.com, page: 93 inset; Don Pitcher/AlaskaStock.com, page: 74; © Hugh Rose, page: 77; Courtesy of the Tongass National Forest, pages: 17 (Karen Dillman), 19, 38, 40 (Jim Baichtal), 50-51 background (Karen Dillman), 57, 58 inset, 58-59 background (Karen Dillman), 59 inset, 66, 94; University of Washington Libraries, Special Collections, UW8122, page: 53; Courtesy of the USDA Forest Service, Alaska Region, page: 62; Mary Ann Vavrik/AlaskaStock.com, page: 21 inset

**Art Direction and Design:** Chris Byrd, Debbie Whitecar

**Illustrations:** Kathy Lepley

**Map:** Satellite image courtesy of NASA/Modis http://gina.alaska.edu

**Editor:** Jill Brubaker

**Project Coordinator:** Lisa Oakley

**Forest Service Coordinator:** Faith L. Duncan

ISBN: 978-0-930931-98-8

Copyright 2011 Alaska Geographic. All rights reserved.

Printed in China.

Alaska Geographic
www.alaskageographic.org
Anchorage, Alaska

---

Library of Congress Cataloging-in-Publication Data

Romano-Lax, Andromeda, 1970-
 Tongass National Forest : a temperate rainforest in transition / by Andromeda Romano-Lax.
   p. cm.
 ISBN 978-0-930931-98-8
 1. Tongass National Forest (Alaska)--History. 2. Natural history--Alaska--Tongass National Forest. 3. Tongass National Forest (Alaska)--Environmental conditions. 4. Nature--Effect of human beings on--Alaska--Tongass National Forest. 5. Human ecology--Alaska--Tongass National Forest. I. Title.
 F912.T64R66 2011
 979.8'3--dc22
                    2011013636

# TONGASS NATIONAL FOREST
## *A Temperate Rainforest in Transition*

Map  1

Introduction: A Dynamic Forest  4

Ground Story: The Natural Setting  12

The World Beneath  38

Middle Story: History and Communities  46

Great Migrations and Global Connections  80

Overstory: The Future Tongass  88

Afterword: Transitioning Into a New Century  98

# TONGASS NATIONAL FOREST

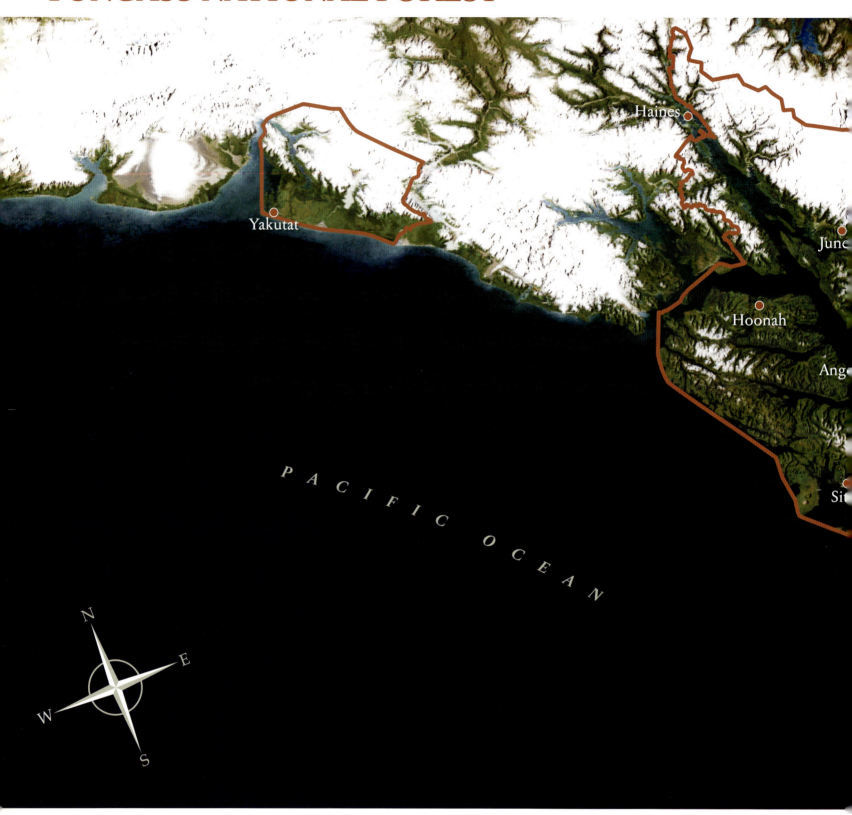

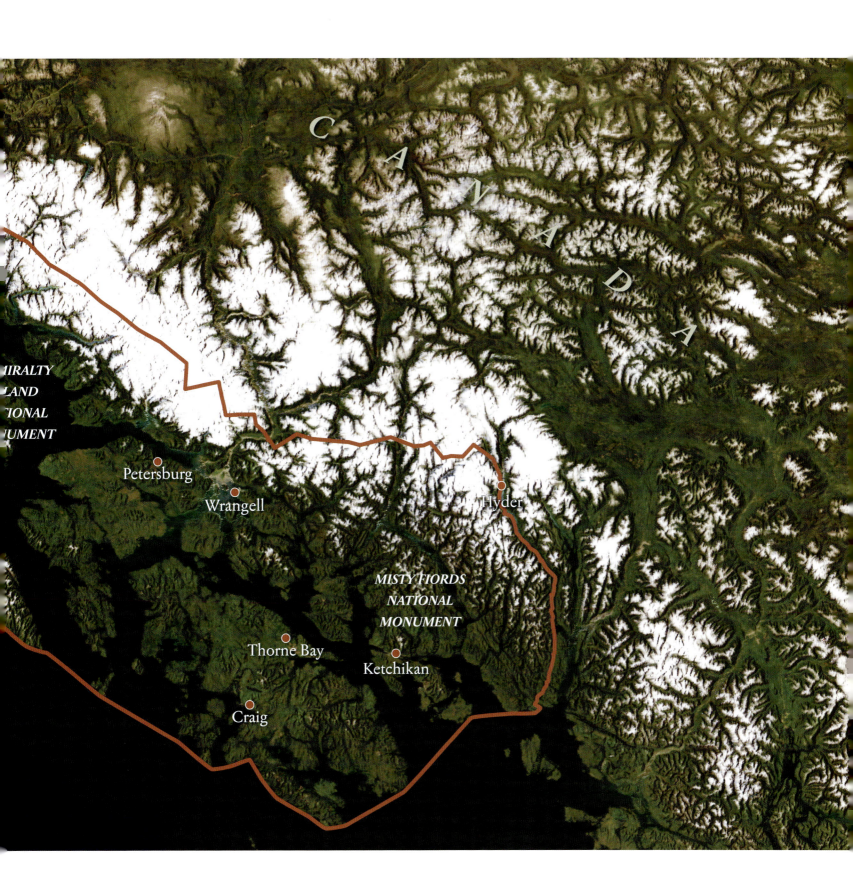

Coast Mountains, near Ketchikan

# Introduction:
## A Dynamic Forest

Stand within the hushed magnificence of the Tongass National Forest, with deep moss underfoot and wet, lichen-draped branches overhead, softly illuminated through breaks in the high canopy. It is a breathtaking and primeval place.

The first words that may come to mind in this largest and most remote of all national forests: Timeless. Unpeopled. Unchanging.

Yet none of those words are truly fitting.

'Unpeopled' is the easiest word to discard first. The Tlingit have called the Southeast Alaska rainforest their home for at least 10,000 years, and more recent research suggests the continent's very first inhabitants may have migrated along these shores in even greater antiquity. All the Native peoples of this region—Tlingit, Haida, and Tsimshian—have a long history of using forest and ocean resources, often in tandem. The weave between nature and culture is strong throughout today's Tongass National Forest—a working forest that covers 80 percent of the Southeast Alaska Panhandle and is studded with 32 isolated communities, where many residents depend on the region's natural resources for their livelihoods.

'Timeless' and 'unchanging' likewise paint too silent and static a picture. Geologically speaking, this ancient place is quite young—recently liberated from thick glaciers that gripped most of its surface until the Wisconsin ice sheet receded. The thin soils beneath today's massive trees have not had time to deepen; the sharp-edged mountains of the mainland have not worn to gentle contours.

The forest itself is constantly changing, both with and without the influence of humankind. Untouched, the forest nonetheless transforms in a natural process of succession. Where glaciers recede or where gale-force winds blow down trees, new growth erupts. Over time, low-growing pioneering plants yield to willow and alder thickets, followed by mixed spruce-alder forests. Fifty to 100 years later, depending on the location, even-aged spruce will dominate; and later yet—after 250 years or more—mature, structurally diverse spruce-hemlock forests dominate the landscape.

Human-caused changes are equally dramatic. From the very beginning of European-American contact, logging left its mark. In the 1800s, Russians heavily harvested yellow cedar from the Sitka area. Large-scale logging that began in the 1950s reduced productive old-growth in the forest by about seven percent. With the closure of Southeast Alaska's two major pulp mills, the timber harvest has declined greatly, but the legacy of that era still lingers in the form of conflicting desires: for greater or lesser development, for more or less resource use. The long-lasting echo of such controversies occasionally obscures the quieter sounds of many people and communities moving on, ready for a new chapter in the national forest's century-long history.

The forest of today is, perhaps more than ever before, undergoing a major transition: ecologically, economically, and socially. Clearcut areas from past decades

A Dynamic Forest

Understory, Trap Bay, Tenakee Inlet

Revillagigedo Island

# A Dynamic Forest

are maturing into young, even-aged stands of trees that may, in a few decades more, represent the future's timber supply. Communities that lost jobs when the large-scale timber era ended have turned to other sources of income. In so doing, they are becoming more diversified and more resilient in the process. Logging is being redefined as smaller-scale operations reconfigure their mills to accommodate high-value timber products.

Researchers and managers, in response to federal requirements and the Forest Service's own stewardship mission, are learning more about the habitat needs of old-growth dependent species. An era of conflict, marked by lawsuits, is yielding by necessity to an era of communication, cooperation, and transparency, as forest stakeholders seek common ground in how the future forest should be managed.

If any doubt remains that the forest will continue changing, one needs only look at how much forest management ideas have changed since 1907, when the Tongass National Forest was first proclaimed. Philosophically, the trend has been from emphasis on a single extractable resource to a multiple-use ethic, to new concepts of wilderness appreciation and protection that favor leaving some landscapes in a completely natural state. Those different ideas are far from resolved, and may continue to inspire future debates.

Meanwhile, the science behind forestry has changed just as much. Even though conducted with the best of intentions, some of the assumptions fostered by early forestry science were unsuited to the complexities posed in Alaska, in part because these ideas had their roots in research conducted further south, in less pristine places, and with different natural conditions. Prior to the 1970s, it was assumed that clearcuts would be advantageous to Sitka black-tailed deer and bear, for example. The removal of trees would allow new growth and increased forage for many species. It's now understood that the habitat picture is more complicated. Forage may improve at first, only to decline as young-growth stands (trees that have regenerated naturally or been planted after cutting or a natural disturbance) become more dense and shade the understory.

What was once considered "overmature" or "decadent" in the old-growth forest is now better recognized for its habitat value. Eagles nest in deformed spruce-tops. Many animals build nests and dens in standing snags. New saplings emerge from the moist, rotting wood of fallen nurse trees.

What looks messy is often essential. Natural blockages in streams help young fish by slowing the current. Leaves and branches add needed nutrients to salmon streams. Even diseased trees have a role to play in the ecosystem. Ideas about young-growth forests have been tested as well. The future of restoration forestry includes the work of scientists finding new ways to manage young growth stands of different ages, enhance streams or improve fish passage interrupted by road development, for example.

At 16.8 million acres, the Tongass National Forest is the largest remaining temperate rainforest in the world. Nearly 500 miles long, it stretches from Yakutat Bay to Portland Canal. Bounded on the west by the Pacific Ocean and to the east by the Coast Mountains and the U.S.-Canada border, it includes 19 areas of protected wilderness, together covering an area larger than the state of New Hampshire, or about one-third of the total Tongass.

With 11,000 miles of shoreline, the Tongass is as much a seascape as landscape: a world of islands, waterways, and tide-washed beaches along which marine and terrestrial life overlap. It includes places rarely visited and places—like extensive cave systems—only recently discovered.

This is the story of that forest: How it came to be and how it has been shaped by natural and human forces, including the force of public opinion. The Tongass is home to 69,000 residents, but it receives more than ten times that number of visitors, and beyond that, captures the attention of millions of Americans who may never visit Alaska, but still care deeply about the Tongass's future. Perhaps no other national forest—or public land—has been so fervently debated and remains so carefully watched. ■

A Dynamic Forest

Nurse tree, Montana Creek

Fireweed, Mendenhall Glacier

# Ground Story: The Natural Setting

Begin with the word "rainforest."

If you imagine the Tongass as forest—the second part of that compound word—you will be right just over half of the time, given that the rest of the national forest is actually unforested muskeg, meadow, ice, water, and rock.

Choose to begin, instead, with the first part of that compound word, "rain," and you will envision one of the national forest's most ubiquitous features: Precipitation.

Like schooling fish amassing before an inland migration, moisture gathers in the Gulf of Alaska, to the west—a low-pressure collecting area that absorbs warm moist air from tropical latitudes. Approaching the coast, the moisture paints the landscape with a soft grey brush.

Fog moves up narrow passages and traces lines between steep stands of dark green trees. Clouds act as an insulating blanket, protecting the land from the extreme cold this latitude would otherwise experience. Moving onshore, moisture is forced to climb as it meets Southeast Alaska's sheer topography. Condensing and cooling as it rises, it soaks or—temperature depending—cloaks the land.

*Rain, snow, and fog shape the Tongass—part of the Pacific Northwest temperate rainforest which extends from Northern California to Kodiak Island, Alaska.*

For much of the year, this persistent moisture takes the form of a light, cool drizzle, dimpling the surface of salmon-filled streams. It contributes to fresh rivers that in turn empty into the life-rich estuaries that are the sea's vast nurseries. It fills muskegs and drenches drought-intolerent trees, like the Sitka spruce. It soaks the roots of Alaska yellow cedar, a tree species that thrives in wet, poorly drained areas.

In winter, the moisture that originated in the stormy Gulf of Alaska dresses boughs of trees in snow, dusts the wings of eagles congregating en masse on braided large rivers, and covers much of the vegetation on which Sitka black-tailed deer feed, sending them to search for browse under the sheltering boughs of old-growth trees. It collects as snow that fills avalanche chutes and condenses over years into glacial icefields.

Everywhere, the soft touch and hard truth of precipitation are felt: in the form of both rain and snow, it feeds and scours, lures and chases, overflows and replenishes. The inescapably wet climate affects trees, animals, rocks, and everything else that contributes to the living and non-living face of this fertile place.

How much rain is there, exactly?

By definition, a temperate rainforest receives more than 55 inches of precipitation. The annual average throughout the Tongass is 146 inches. Some areas are drier than others, of course. Skagway's annual precipitation is 29 inches, while Juneau receives 60 to 90 inches, and Ketchikan, in the soggy south, closer to 160. But generally, in much of Southeast Alaska—take Juneau again, for example—rain or snow can be expected two days out of three.

If umbrellas aren't common here, it may be a sign of human resignation, or an indication that frequent wind simply makes umbrellas too cumbersome. That same wind, by the way, is ecologically significant. In stark contrast with most of the world's

The Natural Setting

*Soggy, acidic muskeg covers 10 percent of Southeast Alaska. The boggy landscape consists of dead plants in various stages of decomposition as well as living trees that may grow only 5 to 15 feet high in 300 to 400 years.*

*With potential both to harm and to heal, skin-irritating devil's club has long been used as a traditional medicine for ailments ranging from fever to diabetes.*

# The Natural Setting

old-growth forests, this perennially damp place is inhospitable to wildfire, a key ecological force elsewhere. Here, strong winds play fire's customary role, knocking down trees and opening stands of shadowy forest to the regenerative force of sunlight.

In a 1906 Inspection Report that recommended expanding the size of the forest reserve, assistant forester F. E. Olmsted described the future Tongass this way: "Let the Pacific break through the main divide in three or four big straits making as many islands out of the principal range. ... Add perpetual rain in the summer and rain and snow in the winter and the characteristics of the Southeastern Alaska forest may be partly understood. To be thoroughly understood, they must be felt."

## The Roots—and Soil—of the Tongass

To feel the Tongass, first sit down on the perennially damp, thin-soiled floor of the forest itself, a place that still bears many traces of its recent glacial past. Most of Southeast Alaska was covered in ice until the withdrawal of vast ice sheets about 12,000 years ago.

Blankets of moss on this geologically young forest floor help trap water and easily washed-away nutrients, nurturing tree roots and preventing soil erosion in the process. Within the forest's soil and groundcover hide the evidence of this habitat's many intricately webbed ecological connections. At the microscopic level, the finest hairlike ends of tree roots are covered by yet smaller organisms called mycorrhizal fungi, which aid in the tree's absorption of nutrients and water.

On bare rock, the forest floor itself, and well into the heights of the tallest trees, another kind of life form thrives. Lichens are actually fungi that live in combination with algae or blue-green bacteria. These partner organisms are able to photosynthesize, something fungi can't do alone. Five hundred species of lichens have

While both temperate and tropical rainforests are wet, they're different in other ways. Tropical rainforests have greater biodiversity (a greater number of species), while temperate rainforests like the Tongass have more biomass (the total amount of living things). In the tropics, exotic animals—even the largest predators—are often found in the high canopy, while in the temperate rainforest, most animals live on the forest floor. The Tongass has epiphytes in the forms of ferns, lichens, and mosses, just as one would find in an Amazonian rainforest. Orchids are found in both places, as well, but not snakes. The Tongass has no reptiles.

been tallied in Alaska's national forests, and these diverse species exist in many shapes and colors, from crusty forms covering bare rock to coral-like or beard-like forms covering the trunks or branches of trees.

In addition to being an important food for flying squirrels, deer, and other animals, this well-adapted group of organisms has additional utility thanks to its sensitivity to air pollution. Lichens aren't protected from water loss by bark or a waxy layer; therefore, they become saturated in wet weather and dry out easily when dry or windy conditions exist. As drying occurs, elements and compounds that have entered with moisture—such as heavy metals, nitrogen, and sulfur—become concentrated and can damage or eventually kill the lichens. By sampling lichen, the Forest Service can track air quality, keeping tabs on pollution sources that are local, like cruise ship emissions, or global, like increased nitrogen emissions from Asia.

The diversity of Southeast Alaska lichens reminds us that this temperate rainforest is both a place apart—unique in its particular geology, flora and fauna—and a place closely coupled with the outside world. Global air, water, and climate issues touch these shores, as much a part of the evolving Tongass present as the Russian fur-traders and post-war pulp markets were an active part of the Tongass past.

Moving from soils and fungi into the trees, we meet the species for which the Tongass is most famous: towering Western hemlock and Sitka spruce trees, with smaller numbers of Western red cedar, Alaska yellow cedar, mountain hemlock, shore pine, and a few others. By tropical rainforest standards, it is a limited species list. But what the temperate rainforest lacks in tree diversity, it makes up for in sheer quantity, or biomass.

Western hemlock is the most common tree species by far, making up 60 to 70 percent of the forest. These soft-needled conifers are shade lovers that generally grow from 50 to 100 feet in height and 10 to 50 inches in diameter. They have droopy tops and a feathery-boughed appearance, and live from 400 to 500 years.

The Natural Setting

*Tapering, flame-topped* Cladonia bellidiflora *or "British soldiers" is one of the hundreds of lichen species that grow all across the Tongass, pioneering a range of surfaces from damp forest floors to glacier-scoured rock.*

*A slow-growing mountain hemlock frames the shoreline of Tracy Arm-Fords Terror Wilderness, about 50 miles southeast of Juneau. Here, forest forms a narrow band in a landscape dominated by steep granite cliffs, remote alpine, and active glaciers.*

## The Natural Setting

Sitka spruce, the Alaska state tree, makes up 20 to 30 percent of the forest. It grows taller and wider than the Western hemlock: from 150 to 225 feet in height and five to eight feet in diameter. It lives longer as well: from 500 to 700 years. Very old spruce trees become dominant in mixed hemlock-spruce stands.

Alaska yellow cedars and Western red cedars, while less common, are the most ancient of the Tongass trees: both can live to 1,000 years. Both cedar species have flattened, scale-like needles that look like braided hair.

Trees are essential to the animals of the Tongass, in more ways than immediately meet the eye. Seeds and sap provide food for small mammals and birds. Decomposing leaves provide nutrients to soil and streams that in turn serve as nurseries for insects and fish. But the trees are more than food providers, more even than shelter providers. They're also regulators. Dead or alive, they affect everything around them. Their size, shape, and relative position—whether standing or fallen, on dry land or across water— determine how fast a stream current flows; whether a river bank will remain firm or crumble; how much sunlight will reach the forest floor and therefore what plants will grow.

The trees themselves are shaped by the land—soil, slope, and many other factors—with nearly endless variations. The older the stand of trees, the more variety enters the picture. Some trees reach only modest heights while other giants—"legacy trees"—persevere into old age.

It's worth repeating that bastions of big trees—the old-growth stands—are only one kind of habitat in the ecosystem mosaic of the national forest. But old-growth has become rare in a deforesting world. The places where the biggest, oldest trees grow are the same places that have attracted most of the historical harvest; the places where the highest-value, low-elevation timber is still found;

Just one of the forest's many unusual plants, dwarf mistletoe is a parasite that attacks mostly Western hemlock at lower elevations. At the heart of the plant's amazing dispersal strategy is a slowly developing, berry-like fruit that reaches maturity in September or October. With a sudden cold snap, the plant releases its seeds in explosive shots that reach speeds of up to 60 miles per hour and scatter the sticky seeds as far as 40 feet. Parasite-infected trees develop abnormal 'witches' broom' branch growth. While a sign of disease, the growths are beneficial for some tree-denning animals, including northern flying squirrels.

Near Montana Creek, Juneau

# Layers and Light

The temperate rainforest is a fascinating world of layers and of light. Starting from the bottom, the ground story or forest floor is characterized by mosses, ferns, and other ground-hugging vegetation, like fern-leaf goldthread, five-leaf bramble, and bunchberry. Fallen or "nurse" trees provide animal homes and nutrient reservoirs for sprouting plants. In spring, skunk cabbage—an important source of post-winter nutrition for Sitka black-tailed deer—erupts from the wet forest floor.

The middle or understory is where the greatest plant diversity is found. Here, from knee to eye level, are key insect habitats and the shrubs that provide food for much forest wildlife. Bears, birds, and red squirrels feed on the middle story's many berries, including blueberries, and huckleberries. With the long hours of summer, the spiny leaves of devil's club grow large. Standing dead trees provide nesting cavities for birds.

Higher up, from 100 to 180 feet, is the overstory or canopy, where the crowns of tall trees intercept snow, keeping areas cleared below, so that deer and other browsing animals can feed. In a mature forest of multiaged trees, the canopy is uneven. Marbled murrelets, a reclusive, fish-eating bird, travel inland to build nests in the high, mossy crowns of old trees.

Permeating all these layers are shafts of light, the soft, angled, ever-shifting light that lends the forest its transcendent beauty. Ecologically, this light is a principle limiting factor for plant growth. Gaps allow for increased sunlight, which in turn promotes plant growth on the forest floor. Total open sun after timber harvesting promotes a profusion of conifer growth; these trees grow at relatively equal rates. Eventually, even-aged conifer trees shut out sunlight to the forest floor. In 30 years, this results in a young growth forest that is shadier and less hospitable to some animals. Left to nature, old-growth canopy with a multiaged understory takes 250 or more years to reestablish.

places that fill visitors with awe; and the places by which the forest's natural health is often gauged.

Old-growth forest is not necessarily the most biologically productive of ecosystems—that honor goes to places like the salt marsh. And yet, components of old-growth are essential at particular times to particular animals. Animals which, in turn, play significant roles in the interconnected web of species which call this place home.

## Gliders, Browsers, and Hunters: Old-Growth Connections

The northern flying squirrel is one of the most unusual and elusive of Southeast Alaska mammals. A nocturnal creature with large eyes and silky fur, the flying squirrel uses the parachute-like skin folds between its front and hind legs, and a rudder-like tail, to glide between trees. While short glides of about five meters are the most common, these canopy acrobats have been observed gliding 45 meters or more.

Found as far south as California and as far east as Nova Scotia, the northern flying squirrel prefers old-growth, structurally diverse forest habitat, with a variety of feeding and denning sites. Also found in young-growth forests, its abundance may drop to about half of old-growth levels.

One of the flying squirrel's favorite foods is ectomycorrhizal fungi of various species, and one of its unique denning sites is inside clumps of witches' broom. It makes frequent use of hemlock cavities as well. Numerous squirrels will share nests, a social habit that comes in handy during long, cold winters.

In addition to being an indicator of forest health, northern flying squirrels contribute to it. Spores of fungi dispersed by flying squirrels' feces enhance tree health by improving the water and nutrient uptake of root systems.

While rarely seen by the forest hiker, biologists have counted about one to two flying squirrels per acre on Prince of Wales Island, for example. They're an important test of the Forest Service strategy

The Natural Setting

*Rarely seen by visitors, northern flying squirrels are essential to the health of the forest. Scientists use the small mammal as an indicator of whether old-growth forest reserves are sufficiently large, close, and well-connected.*

Once upon a time, Southeast Alaska was mostly ice, a mantle that covered most of the Panhandle, leaving topmost peaks above 5,000 feet uncovered. According to recent fossil finds, some coastal areas and portions of southern Prince of Whales Island remained as ice-free refugia. Then, about 12,000 years ago, the withdrawal of major ice sheets began, the transition to foreshadow all transitions. Flora and fauna reclaimed the land through natural processions of succession.

The remnants of icier times can still be found in Alaska. Annual snowfall exceeding 100 feet maintains the perpetually wintry cloak of the Juneau Icefield, a 1,500-square-mile icefield that feeds 38 glaciers. One of these is Mendenhall Glacier, which flows into Mendenhall Lake, site of a Forest Service visitor center on the road system near Juneau. Another major icefield, the Stikine, covers 2,900 square miles. It feeds the Leconte Glacier, the southernmost tidewater glacier in the northern hemisphere.

of establishing old-growth reserves. By monitoring flying squirrels, scientists can continue to gauge whether separated reserves are big enough, and close or connected enough, to support an animal population that requires diverse resources and movement between areas.

One of the animals that preys on flying squirrels—the highly opportunistic marten—is also an animal closely linked to old-growth forests. A carnivorous relative of the mink, these soft-furred, solitary creatures have home ranges that vary from one to 15 square miles, depending on food availability. Marten prey on meadow voles and red-backed voles. They also eat berries, especially blueberries, as well as small birds, eggs, salmon carcasses, and vegetation. Marten use trees, root cavities, and hollow logs as dens and as resting areas while darting from place to place, trying to avoid predation by large carnivores and birds of prey.

Larger and far more frequently seen, the Sitka black-tailed deer is an important big game animal upon which many people depend for both subsistence and recreational hunting. It's also yet another mammal that is both affected by—and affects—forest health in ways that biologists have spent decades understanding. Perhaps more than any other common regional animal, it reflects the ecological links between an old-growth dependent species and a forest in transition.

Clearcuts may temporarily provide forage for Sitka black-tailed deer, although of lower nutritional value than natural openings. After about 20 to 40 years, clearcut areas become shaded-over by dense growth, limiting understory vegetation. When conditions are toughest—as in severe winters, when snows are deep or extend all the way to sea level—old-growth forest becomes most critical to deer survival. The high canopy of old trees intercepts snow, while the mixed-age structure of old-growth allows enough light to reach the forest floor, nurturing the growth of understory forage plants.

The Natural Setting

*Sitka black-tailed deer roam widely throughout the year, relying on varied habitats and food sources. Especially in years of heavy snowfall, deer seek out heavily timbered areas at low elevations.*

*Darker and smaller than their northern cousins, the wolves of Southeast Alaska prey on deer, mountain goats, beaver and other small mammals, birds, and—perhaps most surprising—salmon. Technically, they are considered a subspecies of the timber or gray wolf. About two-thirds of the population lives on the large islands south of Frederick Sound.*

# The Natural Setting

The Sitka black-tailed deer's need for old-growth habitat is just one part of this animal's wide-ranging story. Deer, like the wolves and bears that prey on them, is an animal with a large home territory, requiring not just one but a mosaic of habitats and foraging opportunities in the course of a full year of variable weather.

In spring, after fawns are born and the winter snowpack recedes, deer disperse. Resident deer travel on average one-half mile between seasonal habitats. Migratory deer, on the other hand, travel on average five miles. The distance is most impressive where it is vertical: migratory deer roam from low elevations to the subalpine meadows above tree line, to feed on lush summer growth, and even higher, into alpine terrain. With the first heavy frost, the deer descend back to the upper forest.

Deer populations fluctuate widely, especially during harsh winters and long, cold springs, when starvation is not unknown. During extreme snow accumulation, many deer congregate in heavily forested stands at lower elevations, and some may even move onto the beach.

Sitka black-tailed deer live throughout Southeast Alaska, with larger populations on the islands, which have a milder, less snowy climate than the mainland. But life on the islands is far from danger-free. On the islands south of Frederick Sound—approximately the southern half of the Tongass National Forest—the deer are actively pursued by another large species that also serves to indicate forest health.

The Alexander Archipelago wolf lives on the mainland and major islands of the Tongass except for Admiralty, Baranof, and Chichagof islands. Southeast Alaska wolves tend to be darker and smaller than their northern cousins. Packs of two to 12 animals roam a large territory averaging over 100 square miles. Of 14 dens located in one 1990s wolf study, one den was found under a large log; all others were in the cavities beneath the roots of large trees.

Traveling by boat, most of Southeast Alaska's one-million-plus visitors will never penetrate the depths of the forest, but only see its wave-washed edge. And yet what a dynamic edge it is. The Tongass National Forest has an estimated 11,000 miles of shoreline and over 2,000 islands, from the largest, Prince of Wales Island (the third largest island in the country), to tiny sea-encircled outposts that echo with the cries of seabird colonies and the pounding of waves against sheer rock.

Partially protected from the open Pacific, the Inside Passage is really many passages—a convoluted landscape carved by ancient glaciers and then flooded by rising seas. Tides here can vary close to 30 feet in a six-hour period. On rocky shores, falling tides uncover sea stars, mussels, and barnacles. On muddy flats, the dropping waterline reveals an invertebrate-rich feeding ground for shorebirds, eagles, bears, and more. Where rivers meet the sea, fan-shaped estuaries abound with invertebrates, fish, sea lions, and seals.

Researchers estimate that a single wolf, on average, preys on 26 deer per year and needs a population many times larger in order to survive. Harsh winters and high deer mortality have a significant effect on wolves.

On Prince of Wales Island alone, maintaining an estimated population of 250 to 300 wolves—probably the highest density wolf population in the state—requires sufficient habitat to support 42,500 to 54,000 deer. While not listed as endangered or threatened, wolves are a species closely watched by the Forest Service and wildlife officials. Hunting and trapping, road-building, and declining prey abundance as a result of habitat reduction all put pressure on this species.

While the Alexander Archipelago wolf relies mostly on deer, it also eats mountain goats, beaver, smaller mammals and birds, and—perhaps most surprising—salmon as well. People have long reported wolves scavenging spawned-out salmon, but more recently, biologists have systematically observed that wolves hunt salmon in the way that bears do, though not as successfully.

The added protein source may be especially important for wolf pups. The mortality rate for pups is much lower in Alaska—10 percent—as compared to other places like Minnesota, where half the pups die in their first summer. Further laboratory research has confirmed that salmon make up one-fifth of mainland Southeast Alaska wolves' diet.

### A Forest Stitched Together by Salmon

The wolf-salmon link is only one of many that ties salmon to the biological fabric of the entire forest. The healthy rivers of the Tongass are home to all five Alaska salmon species—king, coho, sockeye, pink, and chum. It's estimated that 57,000 miles of streams flow through the national forest, linking land and river, river and sea. Of these, about 17,000 miles are salmon streams. No other national forest has so

The Natural Setting

*Sockeye salmon in Steep Creek near Mendenhall Glacier flaunt bright colors and curved snouts during their final freshwater phase, just prior to spawning. Just as each fish transforms itself prior to reproduction, all five species of Alaska salmon transform their home rivers and lakes by providing much-needed nutrients to soil through the process of decomposition.*

*Both black and brown bears supplement their omnivorous diets with migrating salmon. For the first two or three years of their lives, bear cubs learn fishing skills from their mothers and some bears become choosy gourmands, preferring female salmon, still full of intact roe.*

much fish habitat, a fact not lost on Alaskans who depend on salmon for subsistence, recreation, and the foundation of a commercial fishing industry that netted 98 million salmon in 1999, a peak year.

Protecting forested riparian zones is important to fish health. Less commonly acknowledged is the effect that fish have on tree health. Salmon carcasses find their way out of the stream—and, in decomposed and elemental form, into the living tissue of trees—in several ways. Bears are known to eat the choicest parts of salmon, dragging and dropping remains many meters away from the streambank. Rising floodwaters deposit carcasses in the same way. Birds and fish-eating wolves do their part to snag and scatter fish. The end result is the deposit of nutrients that break down into soil and are absorbed by trees. Trees return the favor by stabilizing streambanks and shading rivers, ensuring the sediment-free, cool water that salmon require.

### And Birds, too…

The Tongass is home to more than 300 species of birds adapted to the many different habitats found in Southeast Alaska, including not only forest but meadows, marshes, tideflats, and isolated isles. Species include migrating shorebirds and waterfowl that depend on Southeast Alaska's wetlands and river deltas as feeding and resting stops—like the Stikine Delta, which attracts hundreds of thousands of shorebirds each spring. Other birds, like Steller's jays, chickadees and common ravens, stay put all winter long.

Many birds use old-growth trees for nesting, including marbled murrelets, seabirds that nest on mossy limbs miles inland; woodpeckers that pound away at trees, creating cavities that are also used by other birds; and songbirds, including Townsend's warblers, Pacific-slope flycatchers, and golden-crowned kinglets.

One species that requires large home territories in old-growth forest—and a formidable hunter as well—the Queen

About half of the world's bald eagles live in Alaska. The highest densities occur on the islands of Southeast Alaska, where abundant mature trees provide ideal opportunities for hunting and raising young. Nesting in big trees spaced about one mile apart, they'll tolerate crowding in exchange for plentiful food. Two places in Southeast Alaska are noted for seasonal eagle congregations: the Stikine River near Wrangell and the Chilkat River near Haines, where a winter chum salmon run attracts up to 3,000 eagles. Eagles are expert at choosing their lookouts. They build large nests in the crowns of big, old trees—typically Sitka spruce, with an average age of 400 years old.

*The Queen Charlotte goshawk nests and forages in the Tongass, where it launches attacks on its prey from high perches in large, mature trees.*

# The Natural Setting

Charlotte goshawk is a secretive raptor. With long, broad wings and long, rounded tails, this smallest and darkest of three northern goshawk subspecies excels at maneuvering through the dense forest or along its edge in order to capture its prey.

Unlike other raptors that build nests high in the tops of tall trees, goshawks build their nests close to the trunk, on stout limbs, in mature conifer trees. The nest itself measures approximately three feet across and one to two feet deep. Goshawks will aggressively defend their nests, screaming and dive-bombing intruders. Researchers have identified more than 60 goshawk nesting areas in Southeast Alaska, and outfitted many raptors with radio transmitters to determine the size and nature of their wide-ranging habitats.

Chichagof Island

# Ecological Diversity

The temperate rainforest is not a place of high biodiversity, but that doesn't mean it's a homogenous place. On the contrary, what the Tongass lacks in species numbers it more than makes up for in terms of geological and climatic variations, which in turn create many different kinds of animal habitats.

The Forest Service divides the Tongass into 21 "ecological subsections." The variety of these landscapes—to note only a few examples—includes the flat, flood-prone and geologically young Yakutat Forelands, where the land is actively rebounding (uplifting) following the withdrawal of glaciers.

In the central Tongass, it includes the Kupreanof/Mitkof Islands, close enough to the Stikine River to be affected by wind-born silt blowing from that mighty river's direction.

It includes large islands like Chichagof, actually divided into two provinces: a very wet west side, exposed to outer coastal storms, and a drier and colder east side, with a greater snowpack, and deeply divided peninsulas that function, biologically, almost like separate islands.

It includes rugged West Baranof Island Province, where precipitation can exceed 250 inches per year—a hundred inches more than the Tongass average. And, by contrast, the warmer and drier Lynn Canal Province, tucked more deeply within the mainland, and therefore more continental, with less than 60 inches of annual precipitation.

It includes an Icefield Province with active glaciers and lonely nunataks, mountain peaks that rise above the ancient ice of permanent icefields. And it includes the opposite of these snowy, frozen lands, in the form of more moderate outer island provinces—the homes of major coastal seabird colonies and wet, warm oceanic winds.

Chilkat Mountains from Douglas Island

# The World Beneath

You follow a Forest Service ranger up a steep forest slope, by way of over three hundred steps. At the entrance of El Capitan Cave, perched on a hillside on northwestern Prince of Wales Island, you listen to safety precautions, check your flashlight, and zip up your jacket: the air inside the labyrinthine caves will be an unvarying, refrigerator-like 40 degrees.

Inside the cave, one of two that are open to the public, you will be struck first by what is missing: not only light, but also most sounds, and even smells. The ranger points out natural formations, including soda straws, cave popcorn, and flowstone. You take care not to touch the sides of the cave as you walk, not to damage rare features or to hurt yourself with a careless stumble in the near dark. At the same time, you try to feel what can't be seen: the presence of mysteries, of deep time, a distant geological past, hidden in a world beneath the forest.

With its giant trees and venerable cultural history, the Tongass has always had an imposing reputation. But that reputation literally gained depth—both vertical and chronological—just over 30 years ago, when another side of the Tongass was discovered. What began as cave inventory required by a federal act passed in the late 1980s became the stimulus for exciting new discoveries that shed light on scientific questions of global significance, including the ancient history of mankind itself.

Underlying about 850 square miles of the national forest is a cave-riddled karst landscape that is still being discovered. Thousands of caves may exist in the Tongass. So far, about 650 of them, mostly on northern Prince of Wales Island and several westerly islands, have been mapped. Scientific caving expeditions expand the boundaries of what is known every summer.

This new world comes with its own terminology, including one essential word: Karst. Karst is created when rain falls onto soluble

Alpine karst, Prince of Wales Island

bedrock, like limestone. Carbon dioxide carried by the rain percolates through the soil, where it turns into a weak carbonic acid. This acid dissolves the limestone, creating large cracks that enlarge over time into an underground drainage system.

In agricultural areas throughout the world, karst landscapes can pose challenges for farmers. Rain drains so easily through the karst that, despite adequate rainfall, surface soil remains dry. In the non-agricultural, perennially rainy Tongass, karst confers an advantage. Better-drained, calcium-rich soils in this wet region produce taller and healthier trees. Karst landscapes in the Tongass are among the most productive and in the past were one of the more heavily harvested of old-growth timber stands.

Beyond its role in forest ecology, karst has played an impressive role in revealing Southeast Alaska's ancient past, thanks to the tens of thousands of fossils preserved in the unvarying, preservation-friendly atmosphere of the cool, dark, and well-concealed caves.

Animal bones are frequently found in these cryptic locations, either because carnivores have used a cave as a den, furnished with prey remains, or because the cave is located and shaped in such a way that it becomes a pit or natural trap for large, falling animals.

In the early 1990s, the glossy red bones of a Late Pleistocene female black bear—larger than modern black bears—was found in a now-sealed passage of El Capitan Cave. The well-preserved skeleton was dated at close to 11,000 years old. Other prehistoric animals found in El Capitan include brown bears and caribou (neither of which currently live on Prince of Wales Island), red fox, wolverine, and river otters. Previously, it was believed that ice covered the land to the continent's margin with only the highest peaks exposed. New findings suggest that the El Capitan valley was ice-free by at least 12,300 years ago, and raise new questions about the changing vegetation, glaciations, and mammal colonization patterns of prehistoric Southeast Alaska.

El Capitan's first famous bear find is far from the oldest. In 1994, brown bear bones dated at more than 40,000 years old were discovered at Shuká Kaa Cave, yet another cave hidden in steep terrain, and obscured by dense vegetation, as well as fallen rock and soil that had partly blocked the cave's entrance.

Follow-up visits to this small, hard-to-penetrate cave, revealed even more astonishing finds. In 1996, researchers discovered the lower jaws and pelvis of an ancient human, and a bone tool. With the permission of Tlingit groups, work continued. The human remains were dated to over 9,000 years old; the bone tool to over 10,000 years old. Isotopic analysis suggest the skeleton belonged to a young, seafood-eating man in his twenties.

In time, the excavation blossomed into a massive effort, assisted by numerous scientists as well as local interns and volunteers—and attended by worldwide reporters and filmmakers—all curious to know what this ancient Alaskan would reveal about the early human history of the Americas. Most exciting, and controversial, is the support this and related animal finds lend to the Coastal Migration Theory, suggesting that marine hunters traveling the coast—rather than early walkers traveling an ice-free inland corridor—were among the first humans to populate the New World.

If so, those early humans would have been the vanguard for humankind transitioning first into a new continent, and later into a new ice-free era that would give birth to the temperate rainforest we know today.

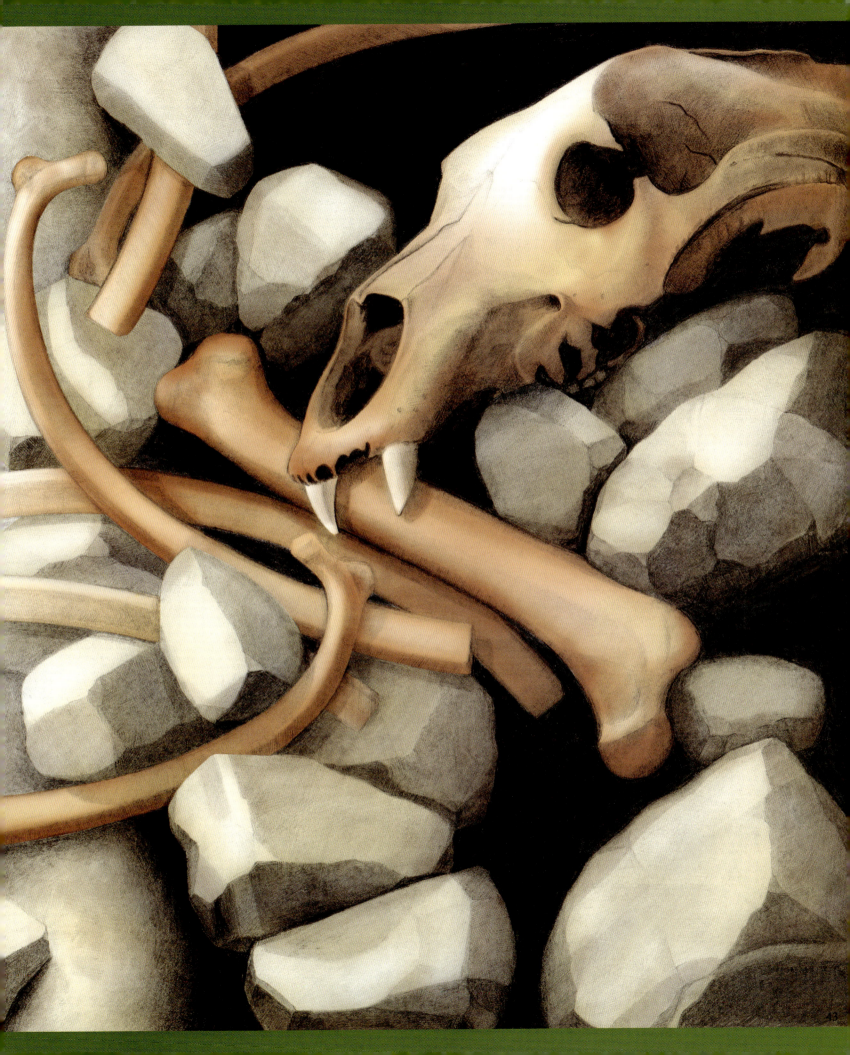

Taku Inlet, Taku Glacier (left) and Hole in the Wall Glacier (right)

# Middle Story:
## *History and Communities*

Every year, salmon make their way from sea to river, delivering the nutrients of dying fish carcasses directly into the root-nourishing soil, linking the ecology of sea and land. But in springtime, a reverse exchange of sorts takes place. This time, it is the trees that—with human help—travel to the sea. And it is conception—not death—that marks the occasion.

For generations, Native Alaskans have used soft-needled hemlock branches or entire young hemlock trees to capture the roe (eggs) of herring. Nature has favored herring eggs with abundance and stickiness. Each female fish can release 20,000 eggs annually, and the more adhesive the eggs the better. Eggs that stick to intertidal vegetation survive better than eggs that settle to the bottom or are swept back out to sea, to be eaten by marine predators.

*Naturally adhesive herring roe form pearl-like strands on kelp near Sitka.*

Each spring in places like Sitka, subsistence fishermen work from the beach or in small boats to trap the roe using weighted trees and branches, submerged just below the level of the low tide. One heavily laden tree can hold more than a thousand pounds of tiny, nearly translucent herring eggs.

Not only is the local form of caviar a delicacy, it's an important cultural food, commonly shared with other families and even transported, via airplane, to other Native communities where the traditional taste of fish eggs is synonymous with spring. Elsewhere in Southeast Alaska, in a commercial form of the small but high-value fishery, fish are herded into pens, where their roe is captured on kelp, for export to Japan.

The herring roe subsistence fishery is only one example of how Native groups today, as in times past, use forest and marine resources to sustain a life from the natural materials of the temperate coastal rainforest. From the time of European contact to today, the human history of what is now the Tongass National Forest has continued along the same path, with successive waves of people making a living from the natural materials at hand. In some cases, the use of resources has been short-term, framed by a colonial mindset that encouraged the simple exploitation and extraction of resources. In other cases, people have done more than make a living—they have created a life, forging sustainable relationships with the surrounding forest and sea.

### Origins

The region's first peoples have lived in Southeast Alaska as long as the land has been deglaciated, beginning at least 10,000 years ago. More likely, humans have been here far longer, as suggested by the finds of human remains, artifacts, and potential prey animals in caves on Prince of Wales Island. Tlingit people tell many of their own migration stories, including one that recalls a move from the harsh

History and Communities

*Sitka Sound turns milky blue with a seasonal infusion of herring spawn. Eaten fresh, lightly cooked, salted or dried, herring roe is widely shared and traded among many Southeast peoples.*

*In ancient times, carvers made their own tools using stone, bone, and flint attached to wooden handles with rawhide. With the availability of iron, craftsmen could create finer lines and smoother surfaces.*

# History and Communities

Interior, in times of starvation, across a land of glaciers to the milder, abundant coast.

Historically, the Tlingit peoples remained an important link to the Interior, as traders. While the Tlingit's historic range covered most of Southeast Alaska, the Haida traditionally occupied the Queen Charlotte Islands in British Columbia and the southern part of Prince of Wales Island. The Tsimshians—the only Southeast Alaska Indians to live on reservation land in today's Metlakatla on Annette Island—moved to Southeast Alaska from British Columbia in 1887.

All of Alaska's coastal Native peoples made use of forest materials, as archaeological research demonstrates. Among the ancient artifacts found in Southeast Alaska are the remains of a basket, woven from hemlock root and branches, found eroding from a riverbank on Baranof Island. The basket was dated to 4490 years before present (B.P.). Another rare find, a spruce root basket from Prince of Wales Island, has been dated to 5300 B.P.

For thousands of years, Native Southeast Alaskans have followed a seasonal calendar that includes the spring harvest of eulachon, herring roe and migrating geese, the summer harvest of salmon and berries, the autumn hunting of moose, deer, and mountain goats. For these hunter-gatherers, trees represented not one resource but many: a diversity of wood types geared to highly specialized purposes.

Alder was good for smoking salmon; hemlock, for harvesting fish eggs. Red cedar, perhaps the most important wood, was used for building houses, clothing and canoes; spruce roots for weaving fish traps and bear snares; and the rarer yew for halibut hooks and bentwood bowls. After giving a message of thanks to the tree for providing its "dress" and with care not to kill the tree, cedar bark could be stripped for use in weaving baskets. Appreciation for and skilled use of trees and plants is still passed on between generations of Native Alaskans today.

# Monuments to Abundance

Picture walking along a Southeast Alaska shoreline, with the sound of lapping ocean waves to the right, and the squawk of a raven haunting the shadowy forest to the left. Fog garlands tall spruce and hemlock trees. Ahead, the view abounds with textures—ribbed bark, draping lichen, rain-glazed leaves—and a thousand shades of green. Against this vibrant visual and auditory canvas, a surprising object comes into focus. Partially camouflaged among the trees, a totem pole reveals itself.

Carved into the greying wood, there might be an eagle, a wolf, a beaver, a shark, or an octopus—vertically arranged images of animals at home in this environment, carved from a tree nurtured by the region's prodigious rain, and made possible by yet another resource that is often overlooked: Time. Healthy salmon runs and other reliably gathered foods provided Native cultures with the abundance—and leisure—necessary for developing sophisticated art forms, of which the totem pole is one of the most impressive. A carved pole was not only a work of art, but a utilitarian object that served to record local history, declare social status, store mortuary remains, or even confer shame.

Despite its timeless motifs, totemic art reflects the impact of historical change. Carving styles, while borrowing essential designs—like familiar Pacific Northwest ovoid shapes—also incorporated ideas, images, and tools from the present. The totem pole's heyday came after European and Native culture collided, as the introduction of steel tools and fur-trading wealth spurred Native leaders to erect increasingly elaborate totemic displays.

Non-natives affected both the decline and renaissance of the totem pole in other ways. Some missionaries, offended by what they interpreted as pagan imagery, tried to abolish Native art and rituals like the potlatch, during which totem poles were typically raised.

Later, federal programs like the Civilian Conservation Corps engaged a new generation of carvers who brought a modern perspective to traditional themes. Between 1939 and 1953, the Forest Service paid more than 200 Alaska Native carvers and laborers to restore and duplicate totem poles in Southeast Alaska, and to construct a community house and associated totems at what is now Totem Bight State Historical Park, near Ketchikan.

The Forest Service recently commissioned a totem pole to commemorate the history of the totem restoration project. Carved by Israel Shotridge, a Tlingit master carver, it was created for inclusion in the agency's "Hall of Tribal Nations" exhibit at the nation's capital.

Land otter pole, Totem Bight State Historical Park

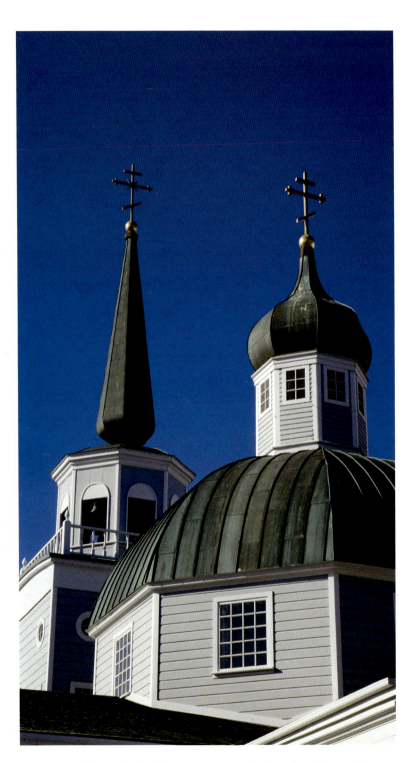

*St. Michael's Cathedral, a Russian Orthodox church in Sitka, is a living reminder of the region's Russian colonial past, which lasted 126 years. The church was rebuilt following a 1966 fire.*

### Russian Era and the Alaska Purchase

In 1741, Russians in two vessels, captained by Vitus Bering and Aleksei Chirikof, became the first Europeans to set foot in Alaska. Bering's crew went ashore on Kayak Island in the Gulf of Alaska, while Chirikof made the first sighting of the islands of Southeast Alaska. Chirikof sent two separate crews ashore to collect water, but neither boat returned, and though Alaska Natives approached Chirikof's vessel and shouted an inscrutable message, the crewmen were never seen again. Short on fresh water and missing a quarter of his crew, Chirikof sailed back toward Kamchatka.

News of the region's resources, especially its valuable sea otter furs, was sufficient to energize future efforts by several nations. Captain Vancouver's charting of Inside Passage waters in 1793 opened the door to other European explorers and entrepreneurs, who established trading posts and forts.

In 1799, the Russian post of Old Sitka was established and a trade charter was granted by the Czar to the Russian-American Company, allowing them to monopolize the area's development. But conflict was around the corner, with flare-ups in violence at several Southeast Alaska communities.

In 1802, the local Tlingit attacked the Russian post. Aleksandr Baranov, the governor of Russian America, retaliated two years later, attacking the Kiksadi Tlingit's log-stockaded fort. At what is now Sitka National Historical Park, the Tlingits gained the upper hand in battle, forcing the Russians and their Aleutian partners to retreat to their ships anchored offshore. In response, the Russians laid siege to the Tlingit fort, finally forcing the Alaska Natives to withdraw to the surrounding forest.

The Russians established sawmills at New Archangel (modern Sitka), and used local timber to build stockades, houses, government buildings, and ships. But at no time were there more than about 500 Russians on the entire Alaska coast. In the opinion

History and Communities

*Sitka, the former Russian American capital, was the site of the 1867 transfer of Alaska to the United States, marked by the lowering of the Russian flag and the raising of the American flag from Castle Hill, on the Sitka waterfront (shown in this undated photo). The ceremony is reenacted every October 18.*

*Perseverance Mine in Juneau, shown here in 1912, was briefly the largest gold mine in the world.*

# History and Communities

of the Russian diplomat Baron Eduard de Stoeckl, to truly develop it into a province worth keeping, the Imperial Government of Russia would have to send a governor and underlings, attract more emigration, encourage agriculture, establish communication, "in sum, create [build up] everything."

Given the politics of the region and the American's belief in manifest destiny, the Alaska colony wasn't worth fighting for. Instead, at Baron de Stoeckl's urging, Russia sold it to the United States in 1867, for 7.2 million dollars.

### A New, Resource-rich Territory

After the purchase, mining, fishing, and tourism developed well ahead of forest management. Decade by decade, and even before the famous Klondike stampede, gold lured prospectors to Southeast Alaska. Gold was discovered near Fort Wrangell in 1861, near Sitka in 1872, near or at Juneau in 1874 and 1880, and at Yakutat and Lituya Bay in 1887. Then mining declined, first with the Depression and even more dramatically with the closure of many mines during World War II. Fox farming, which gained a toehold on many small Alaska islands after World War I, also declined during the Depression, when fur prices dropped.

Salmon was also big business from the very earliest post-colonial days, and like mining it experienced booms and busts. Between 1878 and 1949, 134 salmon canneries were built in Southeast Alaska. After 1908, fishermen began targeting mostly pink salmon, using a newly designed fish trap that was all too successful. The salmon fishery had nearly collapsed by the 1940s and the salmon trap was outlawed when Alaska became a state in 1959. (Despite historic overfishing, salmon rebounded and commercial fishing of it and other species remains a strong part of today's Southeast economy.)

A third industry—tourism—got an equally early start. The predecessor of today's vast cruise ships, steamships brought tourists

55

*The Alaska writings of John Muir and other prominent naturalists sparked a 1880s tourism boom that included steamship expeditions. Muir wrote, "The clearest way into the Universe is through a forest wilderness."*

# History and Communities

into Inside Passage waters as early as the 1880s. Writers like John Muir waxed eloquently in print about the region's glaciers, forests, and wildlife, making it the destination of choice for well-heeled travelers and gentlemen scholars, as exemplified by the 1899 Harriman expedition, a "floating university" of famous names whose later writings inspired yet more visitors to make the trip north.

One of the Harriman Expedition's members and head of the Geological Survey, Henry Gannett believed that Alaska timber would be of great value to future generations. Yet he famously and presciently expressed even more admiration for Alaska's scenery: "Its grandeur is more valuable than the fish or the timber, for it will never be exhausted. This value, measured by direct return in money received from tourists, will be enormous; measured by health and pleasure it will be incalculable."

## The Forest Service in Alaska

Alongside the development of resource-dependent industries, conservation came early to Alaska. The first forest reserve in Alaska was created at Afognak Island, north of Kodiak Island, in 1892. The impetus for creating Afognak Reserve was the protection of overfished salmon streams. In coastal Alaska, fish and wildlife conservation have always been intertwined with the forests, as even nineteenth century foresters realized.

In addition to concern about fish habitat, in Southeast Alaska there was concern for the unregulated timber harvesting spurred by the growth of other industries. Local timber was often harvested for the building of fish traps, docks, buildings, and railroad ties, without government oversight or any long-term plan.

In 1902, a decade after the creation of Afognak Reserve, President Theodore Roosevelt created the Alexander Archipelago Reserve, stating in his proclamation, "…it appears that the public good would be promoted by setting apart and reserving said lands…"

Forest research predates both statehood and large-scale logging. Early forest research on forest reproduction began in the 1920s. By the 1930s, growth tables had been established for Alaska and multiyear studies had demonstrated that young-growth forest would emerge in the wake of clearcuts without reseeding.

In 1956, the Maybeso watershed near Hollis, on Prince of Wales Island, was chosen as an experimental forest, where the effects of timber harvest on salmon streams and forest regeneration could be investigated.

An old-growth spruce-hemlock forest, the 11,000-acre watershed was intensively logged, making it Southeast Alaska's first large-scale, commercial clearcut. For over five decades, scientists have monitored the succession of plant types that grow in the aftermath of clearcutting, as well as the changes of salmon populations in nearby streams. With an eye toward young-growth forest management, they have also studied the effects of thinning, as well as a different alternative—introducing red alder into conifer stands—to encourage the higher-variety forest structure that is more conducive to plant diversity and more attractive to wildlife.

MV *Chugach*

# Ranger Boats

"The motor boat took the place of the saddle and pack horse; hip boots and a rain slicker the place of chaps; and it was much more essential that a ranger knew how to adjust his spark plug than be able to throw a diamond hitch."

With those words, Alaska Forest Supervisor William Weigle (1911-1919) summarized the difference between Lower 48 forest rangers, who performed many of their duties on horseback, and their Alaska counterparts, who patrolled thousands of miles of rainforest coastline by ranger boat.

Since 1908, the Tongass National Forest has used over 70 different vessels as floating offices for personnel transporting officials and work crews, administering timber sales, and more. The fleet reached its peak in 1928, with 11 vessels. In the 1950s two steel-hulled vessels, the *Tongass Ranger* and *Sitka Ranger,* were added to the wooden ranger boat corps.

For decades, the boats played an essential role not only in managing the forest, but also in helping to connect isolated coastal communities. According to Forest Service historian Lawrence Rakestraw, rangers sometimes did residents' shopping for them, and a typical, ever-lengthening list might include everything from tobacco and whiskey to dress materials and baby bottles.

In times of crisis, the boats were to this part of Alaska what bush planes and heroic dog teams were to lands further north. When a flu epidemic hit Hoonah, a ranger took part in a serum run between that village and Juneau, delivering desperately needed serum over the course of a 72-hour non-stop boat trip, made without sleep.

Only Ranger Vessel *Chugach* remains in federal service from the early era of wooden ranger boats. Listed on the National Register of Historic Places in 1992, the *Chugach* was refurbished in 1993.

In 1907, two million acres of the mainland was set aside as the Tongass National Forest, and the following year the two areas were combined into a single national forest of 6.8 million acres, with more additions to follow in coming decades.

Roosevelt and Gifford Pinchot, his first chief of forestry within the newly organized U.S.D.A. Forest Service, shared a concern—rare at the time—that America's forests were not inexhaustible and must be managed for future generations. In contrast with preservationists whose ideas would inspire the national park system, Roosevelt and Pinchot believed in managing public lands for public use—but wise use, in contrast with wanton waste or corporate monopoly. Pinchot, the son and grandson of loggers, supported the idea of the "greatest good for the greatest number in the long run," and believed management should "insure the permanence of these resources."

## The Tongass in Global Transition

The creation of a pulp mill industry was one of the Forest Service's goals from early in the forest's history. In the 1910s and 1920s, several timber-for-pulp contracts were cancelled for economic reasons. As mining and fishing decreased, pulp timber's largely untapped potential remained on hold.

Timber was being harvested during this time, in some cases, for historic purposes. Alaska spruce was harvested to build World War I fighter planes and again in World War II, when the Alaska Spruce Log Program supplied nearly 38.5 million board feet of wood needed to build British bombers being used against Germany. Some nine logging camps sprang up, including one at Edna Bay, which reached a population of 250.

World War I had little positive effect on Southeast Alaska's economy, except to raise salmon prices; population actually declined. World War II, on the other hand, brought both the war—and a booming post-war economy—directly to Southeast Alaska shores.

History and Communities

Cut young-growth, Tongass National Forest

*Between 1942 and 1944, the Alaska Spruce Log Program provided 38.5 million board feet of high-grade spruce to be used for building World War II fighter planes. Nine logging camps and a headquarters at Edna Bay on Prince of Wales Island coordinated the transport of large, oceangoing log rafts to Puget Sound mills, hundreds of miles south.*

During the war, the Japanese invasion of the Aleutians gave the Alaska territory a front-seat view of the Pacific theater of war. Southeast Alaska citizens made room for evacuated Aleutian residents while keeping their own eyes fixed on remote waters, where Japanese submarines were suspected of patrolling.

World War II spurred development across Alaska, from the building of the Al-Can Highway to the stationing of military forces in cities and towns all across the territory. During the war, the federal government spent one billion dollars in the territory, and within a decade the civilian population of Alaska jumped from 74,000 to 112,000.

At war's end, memories of invasion were still fresh, to be augmented by anxiety about the coming Cold War. In addition to this fear, there was opportunity. An extreme newsprint shortage created a demand for new pulp markets. Occupied Japan needed to be economically rebuilt, and one of their industrial needs was wood pulp. By supplying that pulp, Alaska could accomplish two goals in one: it could build the economy and encourage additional settlement of the soon-to-be state, while also helping to rebuild Japan. Forestry and territorial politics went hand-in-hand; the last territorial governor, B. Frank Heintzleman, was also the regional forester based in Juneau.

## Pulp and Politics in Southeast Alaska

The centerpiece of post-war forestry was the awarding of 50-year logging contracts, designed to ensure a secure investment climate that would make possible the development of the pulp industry. The Tongass Timber Act of 1947 authorized timber sales contracts and mandated that 4.5 billion board feet be made available each decade. Pulp mills opened in Ketchikan in 1954 and five years later, under Japanese ownership, in Sitka. A third long-term contract area was originally based out of Wrangell, but due to economic conditions a pulp mill was never built on site. Major sawmills operated in Wrangell, Juneau, Petersburg, and Haines.

When Sitka's pulp mill closed, no one stepped forward to buy the site, which was ultimately demolished and donated to the city. The waterfront site became the Sawmill Cove Industrial Park, home to a dozen new businesses that now include a fish processor, hatchery, chocolate company, water bottling company, and nonprofit educational facility for housing orphaned or nuisance bears. The site also has the potential for developing a deepwater dock.

Average wages in Sitka remain below the state average, school enrollment has declined and economic changes unassociated with timber, like the closing of Sheldon Jackson College, pose challenges for the community. But far from becoming a ghost town over the last decade, Sitka has embraced diversification head-on, with steadily increasing numbers of residents employed and a steady increase in annual gross business sales.

Moss covered alders, Yakobi Island

## History and Communities

At the same time, environmental awareness grew throughout the 1960s and 1970s—an era that gave rise to both the Wilderness Act and the first Earth Day. With this growth of preservationist values came opposition to timber industry subsidies and the 50-year contracts, which had been unprecedented in national forest history. Divisiveness grew as land use preferences overlapped: a rising national demand for timber coincided with a surge in outdoor recreation, bringing preservationists and loggers into the same woods.

While allowing large-scale timber harvest to proceed, the Tongass Timber Act had not dealt conclusively with the issue of aboriginal land rights, which would not be settled until the Alaska Native Claims Settlement Act of 1971. In Southeast Alaska, 13 Native corporations were entitled to select a half-million acres of land from the Tongass, a process that is ongoing. Today, Southeast Alaska is a mix of private (about 10 percent) and public (90 percent) lands.

The challenge of meeting several multiple uses continued with the Alaska National Interest Lands Conservation Act (ANILCA). This legislation protected more than 104 million acres of federal land in Alaska, including 5.4 million acres of the Tongass National Forest that were transferred into wilderness areas. Other features of ANILCA included a promise to protect subsistence fish and wildlife resources, while providing timber subsidies that were designed to offset the effects of wilderness designation. ANILCA maintained the previous guaranteed timber supply of 4.5 billion board feet per decade, a mandate later amended.

Following passage of a federal law requiring national forests to develop plans, the Tongass became the first forest to complete its Management Plan in 1979. In 1990, passage of the Tongass Timber Reform Act posed several new requirements for management of the Tongass act, including the establishment of stream buffers. The act also led the Forest Service to develop a

From the building of the Admiralty Island Canoe Route in the 1930s to the construction of more than 150 rustic cabins scattered throughout the Tongass, the Forest Service has a long history of creating recreation opportunities, often with public help. One of the most recent cabin additions is near Sitka at Starrigavan Creek, where students of a University of Alaska class used young-growth spruce logs harvested as a thinning project up-valley from the streamside site to build a new cabin in an area that was once intensively logged. The cabin is only one part of a larger watershed restoration project that unites several user groups, environmental nonprofits, and high school students in the work of monitoring juvenile salmon, removing garbage, thinning trees, and even putting byproducts of the restoration—like the sawdust left over from cabin construction—to good use as fuel or compost.

science-based conservation strategy for maintaining viable, well-distributed wildlife populations, with a focus on old-growth-dependent species.

Demands for pulp timber had peaked in the 1970s. It declined in the 1980s and surged in the early 1990s, only to decline again. In 1993, the Sitka pulp mill closed its doors. The Ketchikan mill followed suit four years later. Both had been hard-hit by economic difficulties, coupled with the costs of paying for increasingly stringent environmental regulations.

During the 1980s and 1990s, Tongass land managers planned for increased multiple uses of forest resources and provided specific guidance on uses other than timber. Despite an attempt to satisfy various user groups, the 1990s were a decade of intense litigation, with 33 separate appeals filed on the 1997 Forest Plan, followed by two lawsuits brought by environmental groups challenging the lack of consideration for wilderness recommendations, and one lawsuit brought by the timber industry regarding other details of the plan. More recently, the Ninth Circuit Court of Appeals issued a decision finding inadequacies with how the 1997 Forest Plan estimated timber demand. In response to this decision, as well as a five-year review of the plan, the management plan was amended in 2008.

How best to sum up this 50-year period, now drawing to a close? A new state was added to the union, an industry rose and fell, an environmentalist ethic and conservation science reshaped resource debates, communities clashed and later began working collaboratively to address resource management issues. A century after Roosevelt's proclamation and a half-century after the first large timber sales, the forest itself is still largely intact and despite the transformation of the timber industry, it is still a working forest. The Tongass is a place where people earn their living, if not from the trees themselves, then from fish, minerals, and even the wilderness scenery that Henry Gannett predicted, a century ago, would be so valuable today.

History and Communities

*Sunset view from a rocky ridge above Juneau Icefield, the fifth largest icefield in North America. An attraction for tourists and mountaineers, the icefield has also been the site of a major glacier monitoring program since 1946.*

*In a single net, a purse seiner nets thousands of salmon—only a fraction of the annual Alaska catch of about 20 million salmon, all nurtured by healthy rivers and shorelines.*

# History and Communities

Visitors come to see magnificent views little-changed since Gannett's day, but also to kayak, camp, or rent public cabins; to touch ancient ice and learn about traditional cultures; to hunt for Sitka black-tailed deer, black and brown bear; to fish for salmon and trout, halibut and rockfish, and many other freshwater and saltwater species. Just getting from place to place—by private vessel, state ferry, or small plane—is an adventure, as is sharing trails with grizzlies, moose, wolves, and other large animals rarely seen in other states. In a lifetime, even local residents can't see or do it all.

## Few Roads; Lots of Freedom

Juneau, the state capital, has no roads connecting to the Interior. In fact, only three of the region's 32 communities—Hyder, Haines, and Skagway—connect inland by road. Only eight communities have a population of over 1,000, and the smallest of these have no ferry service, no schools, no shopping malls, and no 24-hour supermarkets.

Why focus on what these Alaska communities lack? To understand better the incredible value at the other end of the lifestyle scale: the reason why people choose to live in a place where transportation, infrastructure, and everyday errands can be a challenge. The Tongass, as well as the marine environment beyond, is a large part of that answer.

Unique in its ecology and climate, the Tongass is equally unique in its population, settled in small communities that are both isolated—and connected—by the sea. This is a place where people still travel by skiff to the grocery store. It is a place where school teams travel by state ferry to sporting events. It is place where hunting, fishing, and plant gathering are the norm.

State records from the 1990s show that in Southeast, each person consumes about 178 pounds per year—about one-half pound per day—of local subsistence-harvested foods. That's about nine

Black bear sow and cub

# Living with Bears

To have a bear encounter in the Tongass National Forest, one need not go far. From Admiralty Island to the urban streets of Juneau, there are few places in all of Southeast Alaska where brown and black bears do not walk, feed, and occasionally cross paths with humans. For Southeast residents, the presence of bears affects everything from how garbage is stored to where pets are chained and whether one chooses to take an evening stroll on the community boardwalk. But living alongside bears is not necessarily a nuisance; for some, it is merely a fact of life, for others a thrill or even a sacred privilege.

Of all the Tongass vertebrates, the brown bear and the wolf have the largest home ranges. In the case of the omnivorous bear, that means roaming many miles throughout the year, heading to streams to prey on salmon, to high meadows to gorge on grasses and sedges, along forest paths rich with berries, and to the shoreline, where the falling tide reveals yet more sources of vitamins and protein.

There are roughly 6,000 to 8,000 brown bears between Ketchikan and Yakutat, and about twice that number of black bears. Brown bear density is extremely high on Admiralty Island, known in Tlingit as "Kootznoowoo," or Fortress of the Bear. With 1,600 bears—or about one brown bear per square mile—Admiralty Island has more than all the brown bears in the Lower 48 states combined.

More than 90 percent of Admiralty Island was added to the National Wilderness Preservation System in 1980. Admiralty's Pack Creek has been a famous bear-viewing destination since at least the 1930s. At the creek's mouth, a 400-acre mud flat becomes an intertidal seafood buffet for brown bears. Permits are required to visit Pack Creek in the summer season.

Black bears are the primary attraction at Anan Creek, another famous and historic bear-viewing site, where people have been gathering for a century to watch bears congregate to catch pink salmon. Brown bears also live in the area, but they're less commonly seen.

Brent Cole of Craig makes thousands of guitar and violin faces, piano soundboards, and more from old, straight-grained spruce, most of it salvaged. Music instrument makers comprise almost 80 percent of national forest micro-sales that allow purchasers to salvage dead logs within a short range of established roads.

times as much subsistence food as is eaten in the state's largest city, Anchorage.

The saying "When the tide is out, the table is set," reflects a way of life that began with Alaska Natives and continues today among many rural dwellers, of varying cultures and backgrounds. Anthropologist, nature writer, and avid deer hunter Richard Nelson echoes the sentiments of many of his subsistence-oriented Southeast Alaska neighbors when he writes, "I've poured my heart into this island, I have a strong sense of belonging here, and I think of myself as a member of its living community. In common with the other animals, I take food from this place to nourish my body, and I come here to nourish my spirit as well."

The life of a forest ranger here has its own special flavor in the Alaska rainforest as well. Rangers are trained in bear safety and frequently travel by small bush plane. Kayak crews with two to eight members each, help manage the Misty Fiords National Monument Wilderness near Ketchikan and the Tracy Arm-Fords Terror Wilderness south of Juneau.

As much as these communities have in common, they're also distinctive. Yakutat, at the national forest's north end, sits in the middle of a 300-mile wide stretch of dark-sand beaches that extends from Cape Fairweather to Ocean Cape near Yakutat. The town's main stretch of black sand, Cannon Beach, is named for the two permanent shore batteries emplaced here prior to 1943 as defense against an anticipated Japanese invasion. Today, Yakutat is less famous for its World War II history than for its reputation as a way-off-the-beaten-track surfing mecca.

According to Native tradition, the Tlingit village of Hoonah, on Chichagof Island, was settled by the Huna people after their ancestral home in Glacier Bay was destroyed by an advancing glacier. Hoonah has reinvented itself most recently as a new, small-scale cruise ship destination, complete with zip-lines

History and Communities

Forest Service kayak patrol

Wrangell's Chief Shakes Tribal House, surrounded by totem poles and open to the public, was rehabilitated in 1939 by the Civilian Conservation Corps. A gateway to the Stikine River with a rich Tlingit cultural heritage, Wrangell is also the only Southeast community to have been governed not only by Russian and American authorities, but by the British as well.

# History and Communities

that give visitors a canopy-high view of the forest, and cultural performances featuring Hoonah's residents, sharing their own stories.

Petersburg was named for a Norwegian immigrant fisherman, Peter Buschmann, who found a familiar-looking home among the deep green waters and glacier-covered mountains visible from Mitkof Island. Buschmann built a cannery whose fish supply was cooled by icebergs from nearby LeConte Glacier. Enough fellow Scandinavians moved to the fishing town to earn Petersburg the nickname of "Little Norway." Petersburg remains one of Alaska's major fishing communities, with several operating canneries. With a population of only about 3,000 people, Petersburg nonetheless ranked twelfth in a national list of the most lucrative fishing ports in the U.S.—and no doubt one of the prettiest.

## Communities in Transition

Of all the distinctive communities that exemplify both the unique and evolving nature of Southeast Alaska, Wrangell, Ketchikan, and Sitka deserve special mention. Wrangell experienced a two-thirds drop in population when the pulp industry left Alaska, and its legislators and townspeople have been working diligently to reestablish their economies based in fish processing and local ecotourism.

Ketchikan and Sitka were also hit hard by the mill closures, which reduced timber-related employment by at least 90 percent. While each community crafted its own response to the change, they've both emerged as surprisingly resilient places, successfully turning to other local industries—especially tourism and seafood processing—to fill the gap left behind.

Inside Passage tourism has been around since the 1880s, but few could have predicted its astonishing growth in the last two decades. Between 1993 and 2006, Alaska visitorship increased five percent a year, nearly doubling since the days the Sitka pulp mill closed. Over a million tourists, the vast majority traveling by cruise ship, visit Southeast Alaska; over a fourth of those tourists visit Sitka.

Marble was mined on a large scale through the 1920s at numerous Prince of Wales area quarries, including ones at Tokeen on Marble Island. The stone was used for buildings throughout the country, including Juneau's capitol building. Today, Stone Arts of Alaska, a small company in Craig, quarries multicolored marble by boat from various area islands. It ships pieces to Bellingham, where the raw stone is shaped into sculpture, garden art, bowls and other functional pieces, some of which are shipped back to the company's stoneyard in Craig for sale to the public. One of the company's prized stones is called Aphrodite marble for the heart-shaped marine fossils that pattern some varieties. The creamy pink stone has been used for fashioning sculpture, tabletops, and tile.

*Once a red-light district, now the most photographed spot in Ketchikan, historic Creek Street is testament to the port city's many decades of adaptation to change.*

While tourism, as well as federal assistance and job-training, helped Sitka survive the upheaval of the 1990s, the community of about 8,600 people has nonetheless taken a determined stance against becoming a one-industry town. To date, the city has no cruise ship dock, requiring most visitors to be lightered ashore by smaller boats. To keep their economy stable, diversified, and growing, Sitkans have embraced seafood processing, water bottling, and other businesses that make the most of Sitka's access to both ocean and freshwater.

When the pulp mill in Ketchikan closed in 1997, the city lost its major employer and a prime source of high-paying, year-round jobs. But like Sitka, it has begun to rebound with the help of increased employment in seafood processing, wood processing, shipyard jobs, as well as tourism, making the most of its position as the first major Inside Passage port.

Most Alaskans are familiar with challenges to revitalize Ketchikan and Sitka, but fewer have heard of Naukati, a community of 150—or of its most famous product. Remotely situated away from more common economic opportunities, the residents of this former logging camp found an original way to revitalize their small economy: by creating an oyster spat facility.

Assisted by a grant from the Forest Service in 2002, the nursery raises spat (oyster seed) the size of a popcorn kernel until each mini-oyster is about one inch long, and ready for transfer to oyster farms elsewhere in Alaska, saving those other facilities a year in growing time. The nursery can even manipulate the oysters to make them more valuable, encouraging them to grow a deeper shell, for example, which creates a more preferred restaurant-quality oyster. ■

Swamp shaman, Chilkat dancer, Haines

# Great Migrations and Global Connections

Alaska is famous as a migration destination for several large and beloved species, from the humpback whale, which cruises through Southeast Alaska's Inside Passage each spring, to the five species of salmon that travel from saltwater to freshwater, continuing ancient cycles of abundance that bridge sea and land.

But two smaller species, the rufous hummingbird and a small fish called the eulachon, are just as representative of the Tongass National Forest and its air and water linkages with the rest of the wild globe.

About four inches long and weighing a little more than a dime, the rufous hummingbird is a beautifully iridescent, red-throated and green-capped little bird with an amazing appetite. Using a brush-tipped bi-forked tongue set within a long bill, this most northerly migrating of all hummingbirds consumes tree sap and probes flowers for energy-rich nectar. It rounds out its diet by eating protein-rich spiders and small insects.

Like many small birds that don't conserve heat and energy efficiently, the hummingbird faces the challenge of constant weight loss. While sleeping, it can lose up to 10 percent of its body weight, but this loss is reduced greatly—to one percent—when the bird enters a torpor-like, metabolically conservative state.

Hummingbirds are famously active, beating their wings in a speedy blur of up to 80 wing-beats per second while hovering in front of their favorite flowers. But they don't dart and whir all the time. They spend far more time perching sedately on tree branches, ready to defend their favorite nectar territory from other interlopers.

Eagerly greeted by residents at the end of a long Alaska winter, the rufous hummingbird arrives in Southeast Alaska from its wintering grounds in Mexico beginning in early April. The more brightly colored males are the first to arrive, in time to stake out breeding territories, and also the first to leave. Other birds, like the

pole-to-pole-migrating arctic tern may travel up to three times farther, but the hummingbird's tiny size and immense metabolic demands make its journey just as impressive—or even more so. Some birders point out that measured in terms of body lengths rather than miles, the hummingbird's migration is actually the longest.

In decline nationally due to habitat loss along its migration route, the rufous hummingbird raises its young in Alaska's temperate rainforest, building nests of lichen, moss, tree bark, and even delicate strands of spider web.

Another small and easily overlooked migrant upon which much of the spring life cycle depends is the eulachon (often called "hooligan"), a 10-inch long member of the smelt family. Like salmon, eulachon are anadromous, meaning that they spend most of their life at sea feeding, and return to rivers to spawn. One of the most dramatic eulachon migrations leads to the Stikine River north of Wrangell, where the fish gather in large schools offshore, timing their upstream dash to coincide with optimal river temperatures.

The Stikine River is the largest river that crosses the Coast Mountains and links Southeast Alaska with interior Canada. Sixteen miles wide, the river delta contains one of the largest coastal marshes in the Pacific Northwest. The Forest Service manages the upland areas of the delta as well as the Stikine-LeConte Wilderness Area upriver.

A natural and historic corridor for people, migrating birds, and wildlife of all kinds, the mighty Stikine comes alive with the April arrival of eulachon. Traditionally, Native groups extracted oil from the eulachon and used it as a food staple and barter item. Today, people continue to net and eat the fish. As in times past, animals prey on the fish as well. The second-largest Southeast Alaska eagle concentration takes place on the Stikine as some 1,500 eagles perch on cottonwood trees and river mudflats, eating stranded eulachon. At the river's sandy-bottomed lower reaches, the spawning schools also attract gulls, seals, sea lions, and porpoise.

Most of Southeast Alaska's amazing migrations are sources of bounty and cause for joy, but not all. Equally well adapted to long distance travel, invasive plants also make their way into the most remote corners of the Tongass National Forest, where foresters work hard to both track and eradicate them. Invasive plants usually get their start in disturbed areas and make their way into virgin areas by way of roads, machinery, or soil fill.

Alaska's invasive plant problems pale in comparison to the problems experienced in some other states, but surveys this decade have shown that invasives are a bigger problem than was previously thought. Non-native plants already detected in Southeast Alaska include garlic mustard found near Juneau; Japanese knotweed found at remote cannery sites across the forest; and spotted knapweed, sweet clover, and bull thistle on Prince of Wales Island. Reed canary grass has been spotted at over 3,000 locations in the national forest. Early detection is essential to stopping plant invaders before they spread beyond control—one reason the Forest Service and other state and local agencies cooperate in surveying vulnerable areas and maintaining invasive plant databases.

From the happily anticipated arrival of many migrating animals to the troublesome arrival of non-native plants, these spring appearances confirm that the Tongass National Forest, while remote and apparently isolated, is in fact part of ecological communities and processes that cross borders and span the globe. ■

Tongass National Forest

# Overstory:
## The Future Tongass

On Thursday, March 22, 2007, National Forest Service and Department of Agriculture staff sat in a conference room in Bothell, Washington and held a new kind of open house to answer questions about the Tongass Forest's Management Plan. Thousands of people showed up— electronically, that is. Forty thousand hits were registered on the Forest Service website hosting the "Internet town-hall" experience (on a typical day, the Tongass website gets 2,000-3,000 hits). A smaller number of people, from Alaska as well as the Lower 48, posted direct questions that were answered by the assembled staff: questions about the cost of timber production, road construction, protecting salmon habitat, restoring fish passage, the impact of timber harvest on tourism, and more.

*Logging continues to be a source of income and a wellspring for spirited debate in the Tongass National Forest.*

One hundred and one years earlier, and a year before the Tongass National Forest was proclaimed, forest inspector F. E. Olmsted also made a study of public sentiment about the forest. He traveled through the Inside Passage, finding support for new forest reserves, as well as hostility from competing mining, fishing, and trapping interests.

Foresters continue to face a wide range of opinions while doing their jobs. But they also benefit from modern technology that makes increased communications and transparency possible. The Forest Service embraces that change and actively seeks public participation in decision-making. The earlier and more thoroughly Americans ask questions and make comments about public land use, the greater the possibilities for avoiding later conflict.

Besides online open houses and more traditional public comment periods, the Forest Service is taking part in other strategies for consensus building. One of these, the Tongass Futures Roundtable, is convened by the Nature Conservancy, National Forest Foundation, and several other nonprofits. Its goal is to bring together stakeholders to resolve thorny issues and explore new multiple-use scenarios for the forest.

The public's eye is focused on more than the future of timber. There are other resources, including minerals, of equal importance. The Greens Creek Mine on Admiralty Island is one of the largest U.S. producers of silver, as well as a producer of gold, lead, and zinc. But other minerals have been mined in Southeast—and may be extracted again in future, with the right market conditions.

One of the biggest mineral finds was the discovery, in 1974, at Quartz Hill in the Misty Fiords, of a 1.9-billion-ton molybdenum deposit. This world-class deposit is estimated to contain 10 percent of the world's known reserves of molybdenum, a metal used in making high-strength steel alloys.

The Future Tongass

*With nearly 17 million acres of land, the Tongass is the largest national forest in the U.S. and receives close to one million visitors a year.*

*One-third of the Tongass is designated wilderness, exemplified here by the dazzling and dynamic beauty of Tracy Arm-Fords Terror Wilderness, with Dawes Glacier in the distance.*

# The Future Tongass

Other changes are on the horizon. The Forest Service is tracking an evolution toward young-growth management in coming years, as close to a half-million acres of previously cut land (as well as additional young-growth areas created by natural processes) mature. Areas of young-growth open to harvest are expected to greatly reduce the need for old-growth timber and development in roadless areas.

Yet other areas of young-growth are permanently closed to harvest, having been added to the forest's wilderness areas. About one-third of the Tongass is designated as wilderness, from the glaciers of Russell Fiord Wilderness near Yakutat, to the storm-battered islands of West Chichagof-Yakobi Wilderness, to the ancient lava flows and sheer, glacier-carved cliffs of Misty Fiords National Monument.

These are the places where changes in management are least expected—where the very absence of human-made change is a criteria for success. They are what Wilderness Society co-founder Harvey Broome had in mind when he described wilderness as "islands in time—with nothing to date them on the calendar of mankind. In these areas it is as though a person were looking backward into the ages and forward untold years. Here are bits of eternity, which have a preciousness beyond all accounting."

## Mapping the Future Forest and Glaciers

The Forest Service, forest users, and activists are all turning to increasingly sophisticated mapping systems to better understand and protect the Tongass—from its many watersheds to its geologically complex underground karst landscapes.

Discussion of logged landscapes has moved past the simple tallying of acres cleared. Scientists and environmentalists now talk about forest fragmentation, connectivity, and the "edge effects" created by logging which expose some wildlife species more than others, all spatial concepts better understood using maps and the latest Geographic Information Systems technology.

The future of Southeast Alaska Natives includes both traditional ecological knowledge of the ancient past and acceptance of scientific advances, as was demonstrated in recent archaeological partnerships. Comparison studies between the 10,300-year-old remains found at Shuká Kaa Cave and the DNA of Southeast Alaska Natives will continue to shed new light on settlement patterns along the western coast of the Americas.

Beyond the importance of the research itself, Alaskans can take pride in the level of cooperation that made the original archaeological discovery and subsequent research an exciting and hopeful one for all involved. Native elders approved of the research and DNA was gathered by swabbing the cheeks of participants attending Sealaska Heritage Institute's Celebration in 2008.

In 2007, the Forest Service conveyed the ancient remains of the Prince of Wales man to Tlingit tribes in Craig and Klawock, marking the first time since the passage of the Native American Graves and Repatriation Act that remains of such antiquity were transferred to an Alaska Native tribe.

*Healthy trees help stabilize climate in a changing world.*

# Climate Change

Already, there are signs of climate change in Alaska forests. Die-offs of Alaska yellow cedar affecting 500,000 acres of Southeast Alaska over the last century have been linked to reduced snowpack, which leave root systems susceptible to freezing, especially in open, low-elevation areas. The Alaska yellow cedar is rare but high-value, and of traditional importance to Alaska Native carvers.

There are other signs of change. Since 1950, the number of days with gale-force winds has doubled since the 1950s, increasing tree blow-down. Retreating glaciers are another indication of a long-term warming trend, although several continue to expand. Record snowfalls have been recorded in Juneau (2006) and Hoonah (2006-2007), serving to complicate the long-term climate story.

At the same time, the health of the Tongass forest—which is, on the whole, robust—may play an important stabilizing role in the world's climate. Carbon dioxide, the most abundant of the greenhouse gases in our atmosphere and a primary force in changing climate dynamics, has increased by a third since the Industrial Age. Tropical deforestation is responsible for about a fifth of global carbon dioxide emissions.

Fortunately, in the United States, the extent of forest growth has been increasing for decades, with an increase in the amount of carbon removed from the atmosphere and sequestered in trees. Forests serve as carbon storehouses, holding onto the carbon in the form of biomass. As the world recognizes the value of carbon sinks and moves toward systems of buying and selling carbon "credits," the public and private forests of Southeast Alaska may become increasingly valuable assets. Restoring and enhancing all forests whatever their age may become more than just sound conservation policy, but a source of future economic gain as well.

Over the last century, over 400,000 acres of old-growth have been harvested in the Tongass. This represents about seven percent of the original 5.4 million acres of productive or "commercial-size" old-growth in the forest.

Timber harvesting is restricted to about four percent of the Tongass land mass. The 2008 Amended Forest Plan provides for a maximum harvest of 267 million board feet per year over 10 years, a figure which has never been met since the 1990s, when it was adopted. At this level of harvest, the Tongass National Forest a century from now will retain 82 percent of its original old-growth.

Far above tree line, high-tech satellite mapping plays a very different and dramatic role by allowing people to inventory populations, the economy, and fisheries of the Tongass National Forest's northernmost community. In cooperation with other agencies and the University of Alaska Fairbanks, the Forest Service has spent nearly 20 years mapping and studying the movements of Hubbard Glacier near Yakutat. Hubbard is the largest calving tidewater glacier in North America and one of the few advancing glaciers in Southeast Alaska.

Twice before, in 1986 and 2002, the moving river of ice blocked off the entrance of Russell Fiord, creating a newly formed lake that rose to a high point of 83 feet before the ice and moraine dam broke. Scientists anticipate the cycle may repeat itself. If the lake level rises to 135 feet, the fiord would drain southward into Situk River, flooding national forest and private land and damaging Yakutat's world-renowned steelhead and salmon habitat. As the glacier threatens to pinch off Russell Fiord again, scientists have used an advanced laser technology called LIDAR (Light Detection and Ranging) to create topographic models that help managers monitor, predict, and mitigate changes. ■

The Future Tongass

Hubbard Glacier, near Yakutat

Icebergs, Mendenhall Lake, Mendenhall Glacier

# Afterword: Transitioning Into a New Century

Theodore Roosevelt informed the nation, "We have fallen heirs to the most glorious heritage a people ever received, and each one must do his part if we wish to show that the nation is worthy of its good fortune." Many Alaska residents and visitors share those feelings in relation to the Tongass, a forest of immeasurable beauty, abundance, and value. The passionate opinions of all who live or visit here, and even many who know the Tongass only by its name or reputation, reflect a willingness of citizens to be a driving force in the national forest's continuing transition.

But what will those transitions look like? What additional changes will Americans see as a result of young-growth forestry, stakeholder consensus-building, or the development of new industries? What continuity might be provided by wildlife conservation and wilderness management? What new opportunities and challenges will arise, in the form of climate change or worldwide economic fluctuations?

What will the forest, proclaimed a century ago, look like a century from now? It may be too early to know for sure, but it's not too early to ask and to take part in the Tongass National Forest's future.

The country's largest national forest is a place with room for both quiet and clamor: the quiet of undeveloped, pristine places; the clamor of Americans commenting upon how the future forest will be managed and the steady hum of working communities, as well. Whether by standing in the mossy silence of old-growth forest, visiting one of Southeast Alaska's unique communities, or taking part in the bustle of public discussion and debate, you are part of this temperate rainforest in transition.

The Tongass National Forest belongs to you. ∎

Snowshoeing, Douglas Island

*National Forests exist today because people want them. To make them accomplish the most good, the people must make clear how they want them run.*

Gifford Pinchot  June 14, 1907